Minds-On
FUN FOR SUMMER
Enrichment Activities for Children in Grades K-4

By Judy Beach and Kathleen Spencer

Fearon Teacher Aids
Simon & Schuster Supplementary Education Group

Editors: Sue Mogard and Marilyn Trow
Copyeditor: Kristin Eclov
Design: Rose Sheifer
Illustration: Judy Beach
Cover Design: Marek/Janci Design

ISBN 0-86653-945-X

Printed in the United States of America

1 9 8 7 6 5 4 3 2 1

Challenge a child's imagination
And you've opened up a door.
But to keep that door from closing,
You must challenge them some more!

Contents

Using Minds-On Fun for Summer

Minds-On Fun for Summer is a special seasonal supplement designed to increase a young child's vocabulary and enrich your present curriculum. The activities motivate children to stretch their imaginations and practice their newly acquired skills in creative ways!

Each month, you can challenge your class with . . .

- **A calendar** filled with suggestions for fun days that children may enjoy both at home and at school.

- **Poems** that capture the light-heartedness of the season and enrich the children's sense of rhythm and rhyme.

- **A story (or play)** that promotes creative dramatic play.

- **Questioning strategies** that encourage critical-thinking skills in the areas of knowledge, comprehension, application, analysis, synthesis, and evaluation.

- **A rebus activity** that helps children discover more about context clues in a fun way.

- **Shape booklets** that offer a creative format for journal writings, spelling practice, writing communications to parents, and other writing experiences.

- **Story headers** that motivate children to freely and imaginatively express their ideas about various topics.

- **Creative-writing activities** on seasonal topics that encourage children to use their communication skills and imaginatively express themselves.

- **A gameboard** that may be used to encourage the growth of social skills and to review and reinforce skills presented in your classroom. For example, use the blank reproducible cards to review basic math facts and have the children move tokens along the gameboard the same number of spaces as the answers. Or review vowel sounds (c__t), assigning each vowel a specific number of moves (a = 2 moves, e = 3 moves, and so on).

- **Blank reproducibles** that may be used for calendar numbers, nametags, word cards, alphabet cards, and so on.

- **Certificates** for recording positive statements that motivate and excite the children and help them grow in self-confidence.

- **Reproducible notes** that are perfect for sending short messages home to parents or for writing reward notes to the children.

- **Reproducible art** designed to jazz up memos, notes, and bulletin boards (trace onto clear transparencies and use an overhead to project the images onto a bulletin board for tracing).

JUNE
ACTIVITIES

June Activities

Name _____

June

Sunday	Monday	Tuesday	Wednesday	Thursday	Friday	Saturday

CALENDAR ACTIVITIES

Print the following activities on squares of paper the same size as the spaces on the monthly calendar. Have the children cut out the following activity cards and then paste them on different calendar days.

Go to the library and get a book to read on space.

Make a solar system from clay.

Make some Kool-Aid popsicles.

Try to identify two constellations.

Go on a picnic. Don't forget the jelly sandwiches.

Find five different kinds of plants in your backyard.

Pretend you are a space alien. Go on an adventure.

Make a list of places you want to visit.

If I Only Had . . .
If I had a spaceship, there's so much I could see.
I'd travel throughout the galaxy.
I'd visit the planets in the Milky Way
And discover aliens along the way.
On Haley's comet, I'd hitch a ride
Right through the Black Hole to the other side.
If only I had a spaceship . . .

I Think I'll Be
An astronaut is what I'll be
When I grow up, just wait and see.
I'll explore the surface of Jupiter and Mars,
Then travel on to distant stars.
But Mom told me when you live in space,
You have to put things back in place.
She said my training could start today.
I could go to my room and put my toys away.
On second thought . . .

Sky Light
Do you ever watch the stars at night?
Those little twinkling points of light?
They're planets and suns in our galaxy,
And there's so many more that we can't see.
I wonder if we're just a point of light
To somebody watching the stars tonight.

Shoes for Lunch?

An alien landed in my backyard.
Trying to communicate was really hard.
He beeped and whistled and stomped his foot,
While his giant green belly quivered and shook.
I thought he was saying, "How do you do?"
But I knew I was wrong when he reached for my shoe.
I assumed he was going to try it on,
In a wink of an eye, my shoe was gone.
Before I could stop him, he'd eaten my shoe,
And now he wanted the other one, too.
So, there I stood in my stocking feet,
Hoping that shoes were all that he'd eat.
He did a little dance with his hand on his hip,
Then he beeped and whistled and returned to his ship!
Now all that's left for me to do
Is explain to my mom what I did with my shoes.

Minds-On Fun for Summer © 1992 Fearon Teacher Aids

Camp Galaxy

Summer camp. I can't wait to get there!
New kids to meet and adventures to share,
Ghost stories, campfires, sleeping in tents,
And competing with others in sporting events.

But camp wasn't what I thought it would be.
My parents had sent me to Camp Galaxy.
None of these kids were human like me.
They came from all places in our galaxy.

I had nothing in common with these alien kids.
No one would feel the same as I did.
All I could think of was going back home.
The differences scared me and I felt all alone.

There were four other kids in a cabin with me.
I wanted to cry, but I didn't want them to see.
None of them looked like they'd make a good friend.
We'd probably stay strangers right to the end.

A green furry hair ball with six legs and one eye
Sat down on his bed and started to cry.
The kid with gold scales and a horn on his head
Must have been scared. He hid under his bed.

There was a purple-skinned kid with a head like a cone
Who kept telling the counselor, "I want to go home!"
The kid with two toes and a head that was bald
Was unpacking his books and ignoring us all.

To me they were strange, but I soon realized
I looked strange, too, when seen through their eyes.
I had to admit we were all feeling the same,
But when playing team sports, would we win any games?

Minds-On Fun for Summer © 1992 Fearon Teacher Aids

The counselor introduced us, one by one
And asked us to explain what we did for fun.
He said in no time we'd all be best friends
And reluctant to go home when summer camp ends.

The hair ball's name was Fur-As-Ja-Flue.
He could run a mile in a second or two.
Just think of the relays we'd win every time.
I'm glad that Fur-As is a teammate of mine.

The kid with the scales was Sip-B-V-O.
He could swim underwater for a mile or so.
Our swim team would win in record time.
I'm glad that Sip is a teammate of mine.

The purple-skinned kid was Bah-Boo-Rah-Lou.
He could jump higher than any kangaroo.
At basketball, our team would win every time.
I'm glad that Bah-Boo is a teammate of mine.

The kid with two toes was Hork-Na-Ma-Plue.
He was the smartest kid that I ever knew.
On the scavenger hunt, he'd solve clues in no time.
I'm glad that Hork is a teammate of mine.

The cabin was quiet when the introductions were done.
I think we all realized that this camp could be fun.
Getting to know how we felt inside
Was turning out to be quite a surprise.

Then Bah-Boo burped and asked, "What's for lunch?"
We all started laughing and talking at once.
We'd be the best cabin in Camp Galaxy
With all of our differences—what a team we would be!

14

QUESTIONS AND ACTIVITIES FOR THE STORY

1. Who was the main character of this story?

2. Where was the little boy? Where were the other kids from? List all the characters. Describe each one.

3. What is the main idea of this story?

4. Retell this story in your own words. Make up a new ending.

5. Why did the boy telling the story want to go home? Have you ever been unsure of someone because of his or her appearance?

6. Have you ever taken a risk and tried something new? When?

7. Compare how the characters felt at the beginning of the story, the middle, and at the end of the story. Make a diagram showing how the characters became a team.

8. Predict what might have happened to the characters in the story if they hadn't liked sports. If you had been the counselor, what plan might you have invented to unite the characters?

9. Why is it important not to judge people before you get to know them?

10. Choose an alien that you might like to be. Explain your choice.

Name _____

Cut out the pictures below and paste them in the correct boxes.

My birthday  came today from my Uncle Dave. He lives far away.

He's an astronaut and he has walked on the  . He said he'd come and see me

soon. His present was a  about Mars and a to watch the night

 . He sent a model of a  ship and a to wear on my

hip. I saved him a piece of my birthday , but my ate it right

off the plate!

moon   cake   book   ray gun

dog   rocket   telescope   present   stars

Minds-On Fun for Summer © 1992 Fearon Teacher Aids

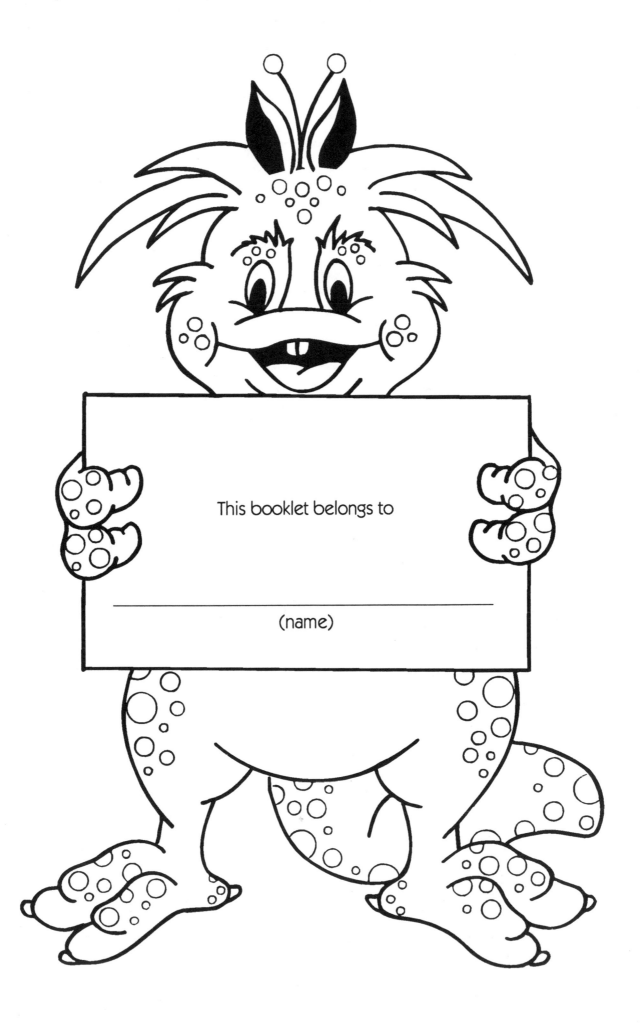

This booklet belongs to

_____

(name)

This booklet belongs to

_____

(name)

Minds-On Fun for Summer © 1992 Fearon Teacher Aids

Name _____

_____

_____

_____

_____

_____

_____

_____

_____

_____

_____

_____

Name _____

Gr-r-reat galaxies! Our space shuttle is in peril. It's being sucked into a Black Hole! There are only seconds remaining. The only thing left for us to do is. . . . . Write what you would do!

Attach to the top portion of your story.

Minds-On Fun for Summer © 1992 Fearon Teacher Aids

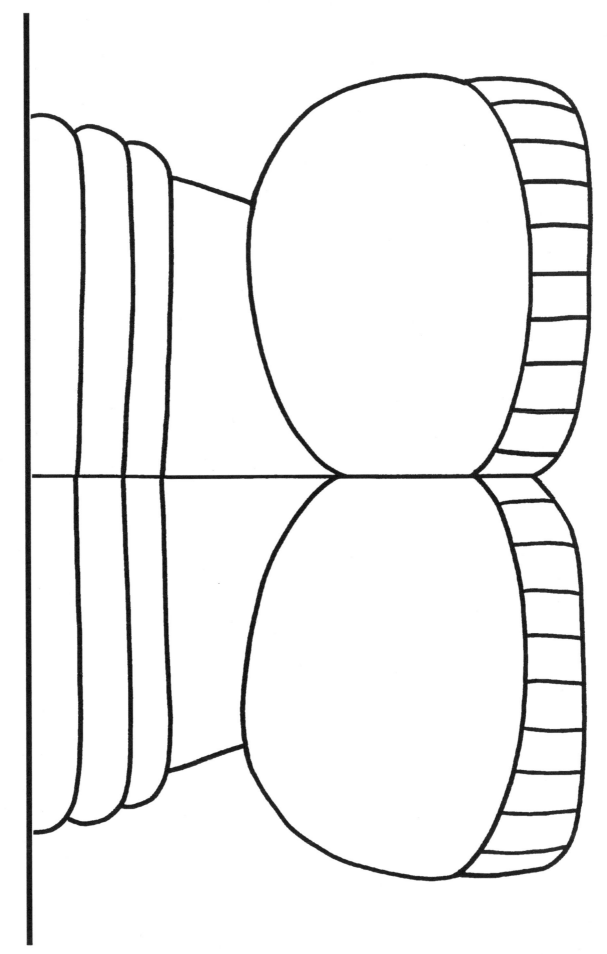

Attach to the bottom portion of your story.

Name _____

Late one summer's night, while I was looking through my telescope, I saw an unusual sight. . . . What did you see?

Attach to the top portion of your story.

The season is changing.
There are hot days ahead.
The apples and cherries
Have all turned red.
The fruit on the tree
Is ready to pick,
And summer vacation
Is coming up quick!
What other signs of summer do you see?

_____

_____

_____

_____

_____

_____

_____

Name _____

My Dad
There's a very special person
That I often rely upon
To answer all my questions
And teach me right from wrong,
To be there when I'm troubled
And explain my fears away,
Or make up funny stories
And games that we can play.
For all your love and kindness,
I'd just like to say,
"I love you, Dad, so very much.
Happy Father's Day!"

List a few of the special things your father does with you.

_____

_____

_____

_____

_____

_____

Minds-On Fun for Summer © 1992 Fearon Teacher Aids

Name _____

The government has asked you to design a space station. Draw your space station in the box below. Describe the power source that will run the space station on the lines provided.

```



```

_____

_____

_____

_____

_____

_____

Name _____

Did you ever notice
When you wanted to have fun,
There were always some chores
That had to be done?
Take out the garbage, make your bed,
Be sure your pets are properly fed.
Wash the dishes, sweep the floor,
Dust the tables, and so many more.
They're all important and have to be done,
But wouldn't you rather be out having fun?
So, for all the duties that you hate to do,
Design a robot to do them for you.

Describe what chores your robot can do. Then draw a picture of the robot in the space provided below.

_____

_____

_____

_____

_____

_____

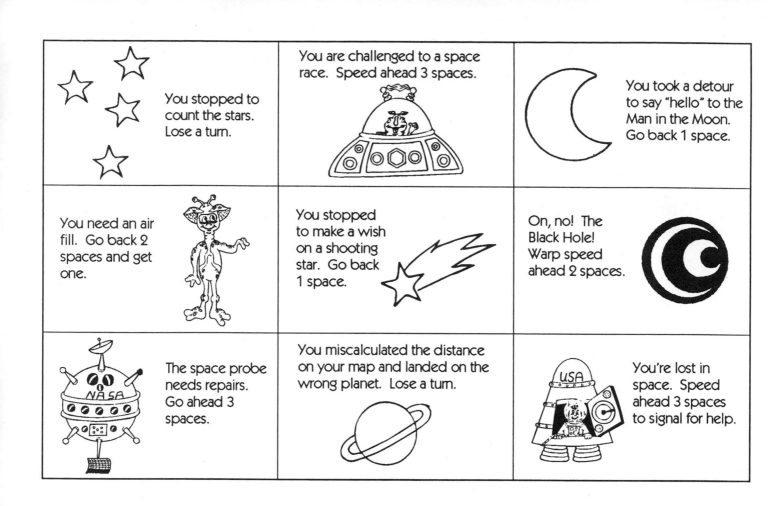

You stopped to count the stars. Lose a turn.

You are challenged to a space race. Speed ahead 3 spaces.

You took a detour to say "hello" to the Man in the Moon. Go back 1 space.

You need an air fill. Go back 2 spaces and get one.

You stopped to make a wish on a shooting star. Go back 1 space.

On, no! The Black Hole! Warp speed ahead 2 spaces.

The space probe needs repairs. Go ahead 3 spaces.

You miscalculated the distance on your map and landed on the wrong planet. Lose a turn.

You're lost in space. Speed ahead 3 spaces to signal for help.

Name _____

Name _____

Name

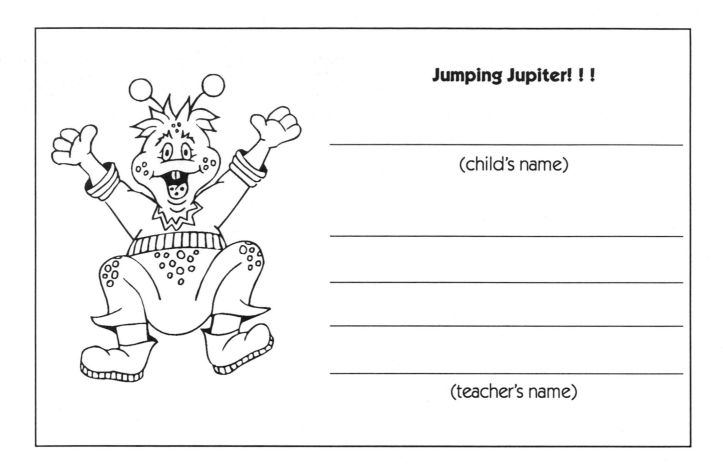

Jumping Jupiter! ! !

_____

(child's name)

_____

_____

_____

_____

(teacher's name)

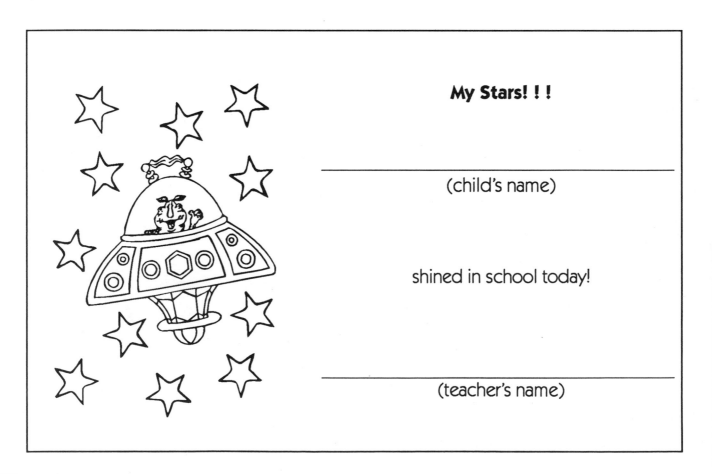

My Stars! ! !

_____

(child's name)

shined in school today!

_____

(teacher's name)

Minds-On Fun for Summer © 1992 Fearon Teacher Aids

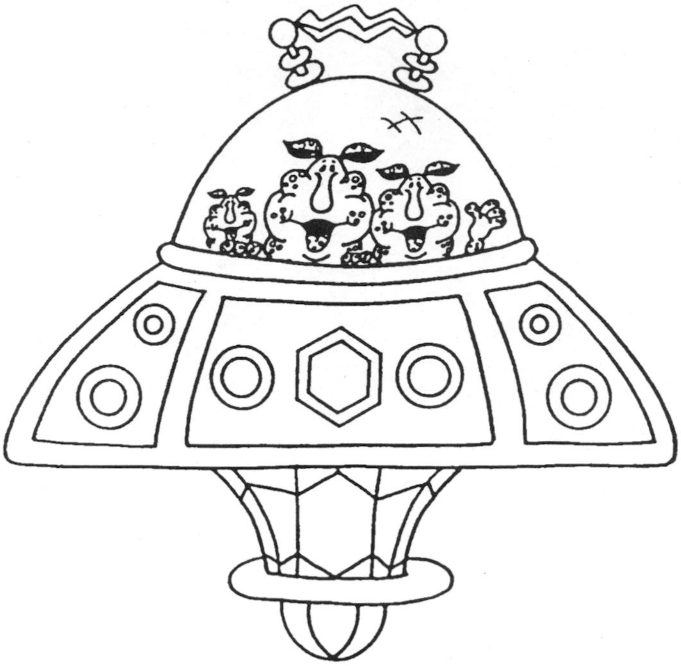

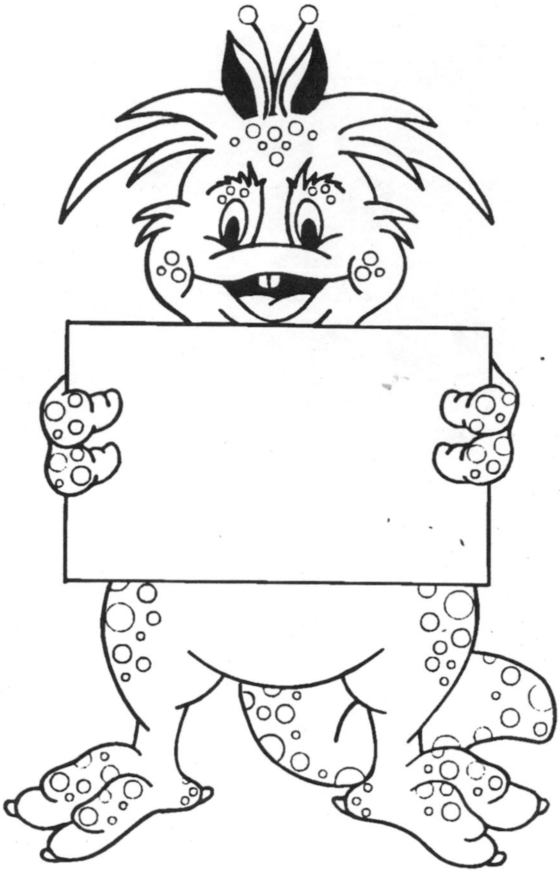

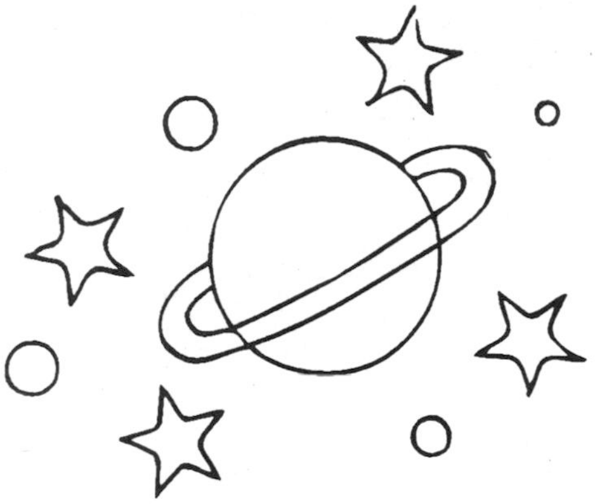

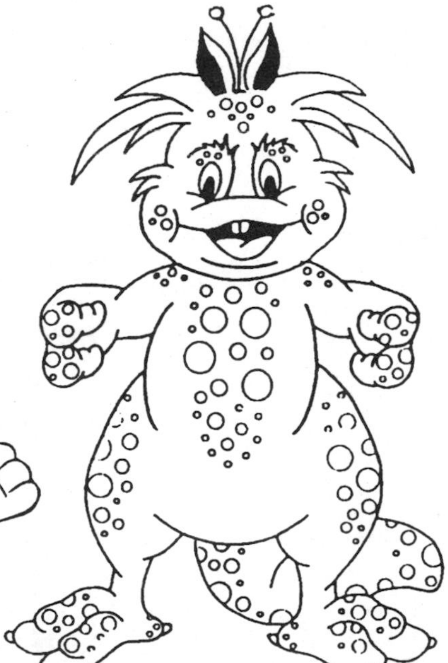

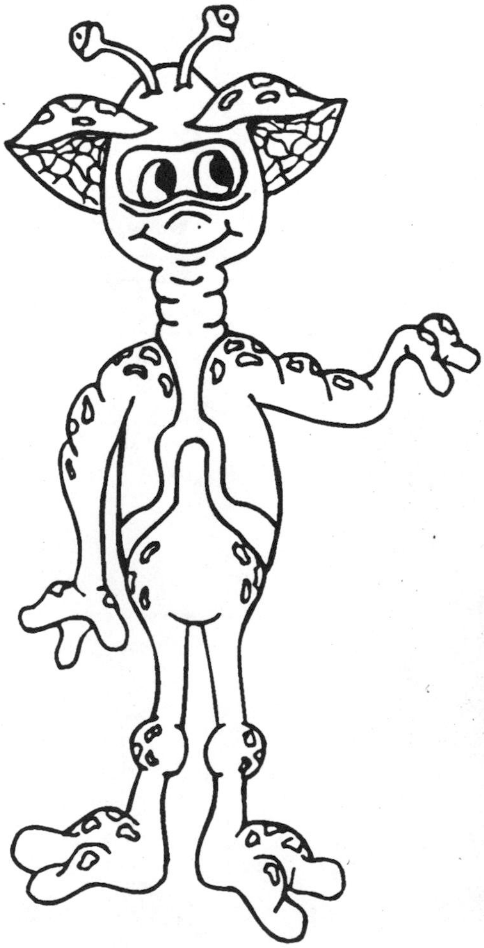

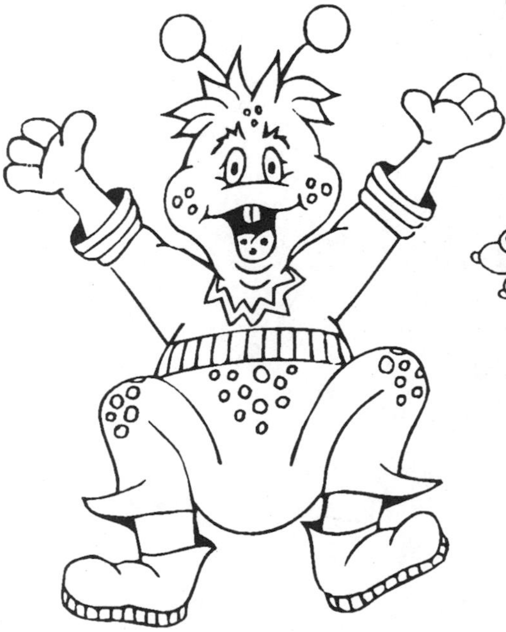

JULY ACTIVITIES

July Activities

Name _____

July

Sunday	Monday	Tuesday	Wednesday	Thursday	Friday	Saturday

CALENDAR ACTIVITIES

Print the following activities on squares of paper the same size as the spaces on the monthly calendar. Have the children cut out the following activity cards and then paste them on different calendar days.

Watch the fireworks! Illustrate your favorite one.

Review the fire safety rules: Stop! Drop! Roll!

Go on a picnic. Watch out for hungry ants!

Set up a lemonade stand.

Organize a neighborhood baseball game.

Go on an insect hunt. How many different kinds of insects can you find?

Help Mom and Dad with the yard work.

Read the back of your cereal box.

Clouds in the Sky

Lying on a hill on a lazy summer day,
Watching the clouds as they drift my way.
With a little imagination, a cloud can be
Anything you like, from a witch to a tree.
The image doesn't last long. It soon drifts apart.
I can even see myself as I slowly drift by,
Lying on a hill made of clouds in the sky.

A Magical Fourth of July

I remember my first fireworks on the Fourth of July.
The sound of the explosions were loud and I cried.
Then suddenly it was bright—night turned into day
From the lights overhead that the explosions displayed.
All I could do was just say "O-o-oh!" and "A-a-ah!"
With the rest of the people at what we saw.
Rockets went streaking across the sky,
Exploding with colors that dazzled the eye.
I'll never forget my first Fourth of July
And the magical colors that lit up the sky!

Back to Class

Summer vacation goes by so fast.
Before you know it, you're back in class.
I think my friends feel as I do.
They all really want to go back to school.
Oh, everyone will moan and groan
And put on a show about staying at home.
But even though we may make a fuss,
We're always smiling as we get on the bus.

Bad Sport Herman

This is a play about Herman and four friends who want to play baseball on a hot summer's day.

Cast:
Pitcher
Umpire
Batter 1
Batter 2
Herman
Stu
Dustin
Belinda
Henry

Props:
Baseball
Baseball bat
Baseball gloves

Scene 1

Scene 1 opens just as the game is about to begin. The team has been told that their best player, Tim, is home sick with the chicken pox. As Stu, Dustin, Belinda, and Henry desperately look around trying to find a replacement for Tim, they see Herman.

Stu: Hey, guys! I think we're stuck with bad sport Herman.

Dustin: I'm not going to ask him to play with us. You know what happened last time.

Belinda: Do we have a choice? Let's give him another chance.

Henry: Yeah! What do we have to lose? This time we have our own bat and ball. He won't be able to take it home when he gets mad!

Stu: Hey, Herman! Wanna play some ball?

Herman: Maybe I do! Maybe I don't!

Dustin: Okay guys, let's go fishing instead.

Herman: Okay, I'll play ball. I don't have anything better to do.

Belinda: It will be fun!

Herman: Come on guys! Let's go smash them!

Minds-On Fun for Summer © 1992 Fearon Teacher Aids

Stu: Wait a minute, Herman. This is just a friendly game of baseball.

Herman: Friendly games are for losers! I'm here to win.

Dustin: (As the friends take their places on the baseball field, Dustin mumbles to himself.) I think it's more fun to eat lima beans than play baseball with bad sport Herman.

Scene 2

Scene 2 opens with Herman being loud and mean to Batter 1. The friends look at each other a little embarrassed.

Herman: Hey, batter! Batter! You can't hit the ball cuz your brains are too small.

Stu: Don't be so mean, Herman!

Dustin: (Shaking his head and grumbling.) I've got a sudden craving for lima beans.

Stu: Huh? You hate lima beans!

Belinda: Come on, guys! Two outs and only one more to go!

Herman: Hey, batter! Batter! You call that a swing? If you keep that up, you won't hit a thing! (Wack! The batter connects and sends a hit into center field. It's heading straight toward Belinda.)

Belinda: I've got it! I've got it! Ouch!

Herman: (Herman pushes Belinda out of the way.) Get out of my way! I've got this one. Oops! (Herman drops the baseball.)

Stu: Herman! You heard Belinda! She said she had it!

Herman: I saw it first! Besides, she wouldn't have caught it anyway. She has a hole in her glove!

Henry: Talk about holes in your gloves. You dropped it, too.

Herman: I wouldn't have if Belinda hadn't gotten in my way!

Stu: Come on, Herman! We need a little teamwork here.

Belinda: Pay attention guys. Just one more out and we're up.

Herman: (Batter 2 walks up to the plate.) Hey, batter! Batter! What's the matter, you got a hole in your bat? Sure looks like it when you swing like that! (Smack! Wham! The batter hits the baseball into left field. Herman catches the baseball, drops it, and throws it out of control to first base. Stu runs after the ball.)

Dustin: Quick, Stu! Throw it to Henry on third base!

Henry: Got it! You're out! Great throw, Stu!

Herman: What do you mean? What great throw? The batter would have been out at first base if Stu would have caught the ball!

Scene 2 ends with the players leaving the field and Dustin mumbling something about lima beans.

Scene 3

Scene 3 opens with Herman up to bat. He swings and misses.

Herman: What do you mean, strike one? It was outside! Way outside!

Umpire: Strike two!

Herman: What? Are you blind or what?

Umpire: Strike three!

Herman: What do you mean, strike three? That ball was inside and low! (Herman throws down the bat and storms off the batter's plate.) What a bunch of losers! I don't want to play this game anymore!

Belinda: Come on, Herman. We're just here to have some fun.

Stu: So what if you struck out?

Herman: I didn't strike out! It's not my fault the umpire can't tell a strike from a ball!

Henry: Herman, maybe the next time at bat you'll hit a home run!

Herman: You don't care that I just struck out?

Belinda: We've all struck out at one time or another. Just do your best.

Minds-On Fun for Summer © 1992 Fearon Teacher Aids

Herman: Yeah! Maybe I'll give it one more try. Who knows? I might even hit a home run!

Stu: That's the spirit, Herman.

Dustin: Maybe this doesn't call for lima beans after all.

Herman: Lima beans? Yuk!

The scene ends as the baseball game continues. Herman's attitude changes as he learns good sportsmanship—it's not whether you win or lose, but how you play the game!

QUESTIONS AND ACTIVITIES FOR THE PLAY

1. Why was Herman a bad sport? Have you ever been a bad sport?

2. What is the main idea of this story? Have you ever blamed someone else for your mistakes? Explain.

3. Retell the story in your own words. Make up a new ending to the story.

4. Have you ever been teased by your friends because you weren't as good as they were? Explain.

5. Compare Herman's feelings about sportsmanship at the beginning of the game to his feelings at the end of the game.

6. Compare Herman with yourself. How are you alike? How are you different?

7. Should Dustin, Belinda, Stu, and Henry have let Herman play baseball with them? Defend your answer. What other ways could the friends have helped Herman learn his lesson about sportsmanship?

8. Predict what will happen the next time the friends ask Herman to play baseball with them.

9. Why is it important to be a good sport?

10. Do you think the friends did the right thing by giving Herman another chance?

Name _____

Cut out the pictures below and paste them in the correct boxes.

Going on a picnic can be lots of fun. You eat on a ☐ outside in the ☐.

The picnic ☐ was ready to take. There were ☐ butter sandwiches,

candy , and ☐. Dad drove the ☐ to a spot by

the lake. My mom had to tell Dad what turns he should take. By the ☐ we

unpacked, rain ☐ had formed. ☐ were falling. We were in for a storm.

We still had our picnic, but we ate in the car. It turned out to be the best picnic so far!

cake   car   clouds   sun

apples   raindrops   blanket   basket   peanut   time

This booklet belongs to

_____

(name)

Minds-On Fun for Summer © 1992 Fearon Teacher Aids

This booklet belongs to

_____

(name)

Name _____

_____

_____

_____

_____

_____

_____

_____

_____

_____

_____

Minds-On Fun for Summer © 1992 Fearon Teacher Aids

Name

"America the Beautiful" and "Oh, Say Can You See?" are songs about our country. Make up your own song about America. Use the tune "Twinkle, Twinkle, Little Star."

Attach to the top portion of your song.

Attach to the bottom portion of your song.

Minds-On Fun for Summer © 1992 Fearon Teacher Aids

Minds-On Fun for Summer © 1992 Fearon Teacher Aids

Name _____

It sounded like such a good idea to sleep out in the backyard until. . . . .
What happened?

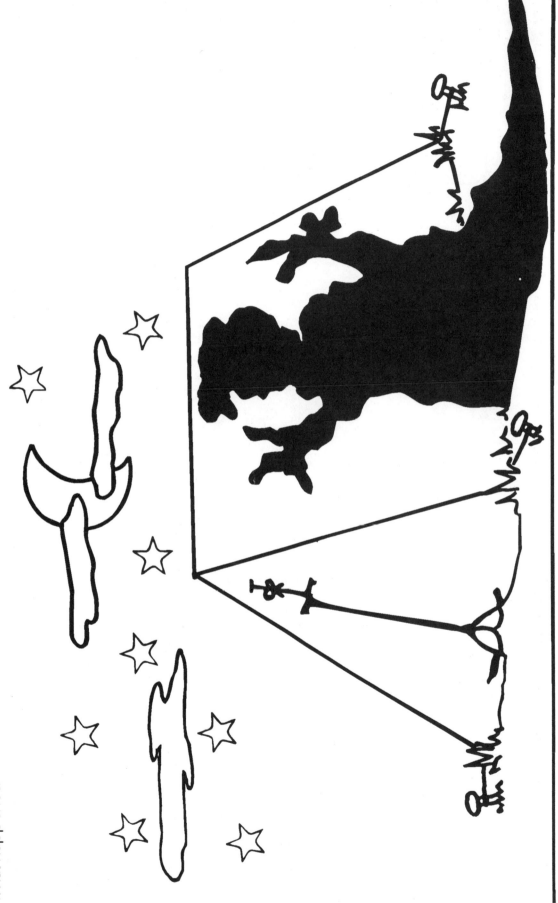

Attach to the top portion of your story.

Name _____

It's July! It's 106 degrees in the shade.
You decide to cool off with some pink lemonade.
While in the kitchen, you think about lunch.
You aren't very hungry. You just want something to munch!

Use your imagination. Be creative.
Create a recipe for a cool summer snack.

_____

_____

_____

_____

_____

_____

_____

Ants on a mission.
That's what we are.
Looking for picnickers
Near and far!
We may be little
But we're well-organized.
We can accomplish a lot
For insects our size!
Teamwork and planning
Is all that it takes
To get around picnickers
And sneak off with cakes!

Pretend you are an ant. Describe how you will sneak off with the picnic food.
Then make a map showing how you will get the food away from the picnic.

Name _____

I went on vacation and while we were travelling about,
I picked up a postcard and filled it out.
The picture on the front was from a state we'd been in,
On the back was a message I wrote to my friend.

Draw a picture of a tourist attraction from one of the states you have visited on the front side of the postcard below. Write a message to a friend on the back.

front

back

stamp

Minds-On Fun for Summer © 1992 Fearon Teacher Aids

Name _____

You're always bored on a rainy day
But it doesn't have to be that way.
Use your imagination. Make up a board game.
Design the board and make up a name.
What are the rules and how is it played?
It's all up to you how this game is made!

Describe your game. Then draw the gameboard in the space provided below.

_____

_____

_____

_____

_____

_____

Name _____

I was out in the woods
Just hiking around
When I tripped on a rock
And fell to the ground.
I opened my eyes
And all I could see
Was a very strange bug
Staring at me!

Use your imagination and describe what the bug looks like, what it eats, and how it is helpful to the environment. Then draw a picture of the strange-looking bug.

Minds-On Fun for Summer © 1992 Fearon Teacher Aids

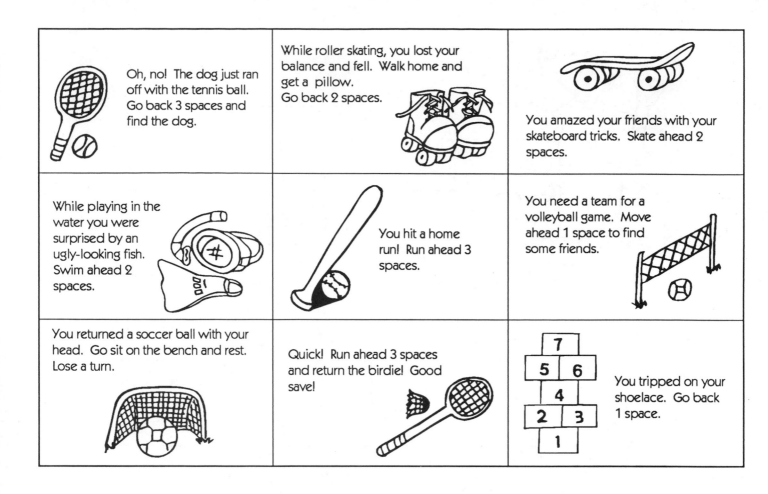

Oh, no! The dog just ran off with the tennis ball. Go back 3 spaces and find the dog.

While roller skating, you lost your balance and fell. Walk home and get a pillow. Go back 2 spaces.

You amazed your friends with your skateboard tricks. Skate ahead 2 spaces.

While playing in the water you were surprised by an ugly-looking fish. Swim ahead 2 spaces.

You hit a home run! Run ahead 3 spaces.

You need a team for a volleyball game. Move ahead 1 space to find some friends.

You returned a soccer ball with your head. Go sit on the bench and rest. Lose a turn.

Quick! Run ahead 3 spaces and return the birdie! Good save!

You tripped on your shoelace. Go back 1 space.

Name _____

Minds-On Fun for Summer © 1992 Fearon Teacher Aids

Name _____

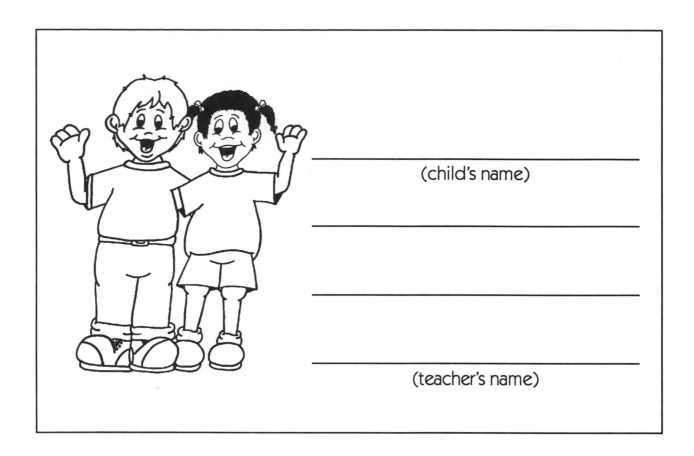

_____
(child's name)

_____

_____

_____
(teacher's name)

Hip, hip, hooray!

_____
(child's name)

worked INDEPENDENTLY today!

_____
(teacher's name)

Minds-On Fun for Summer © 1992 Fearon Teacher Aids

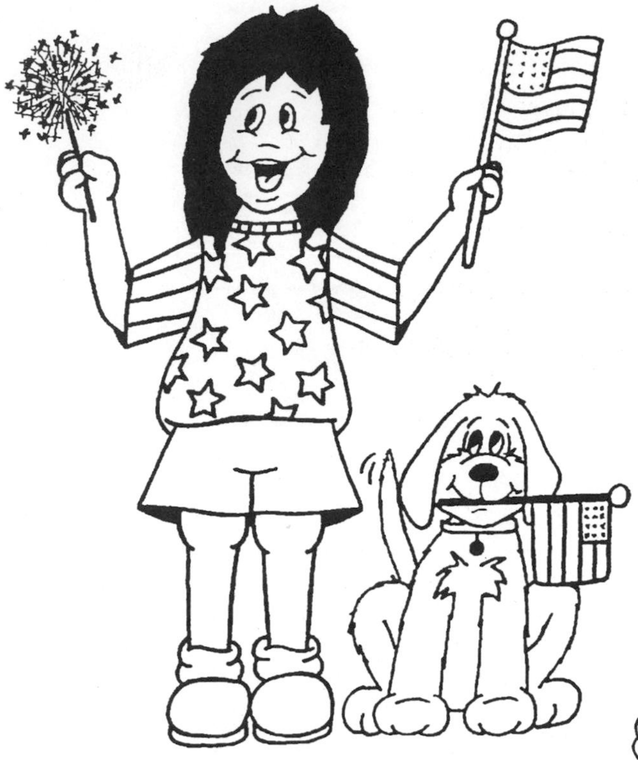

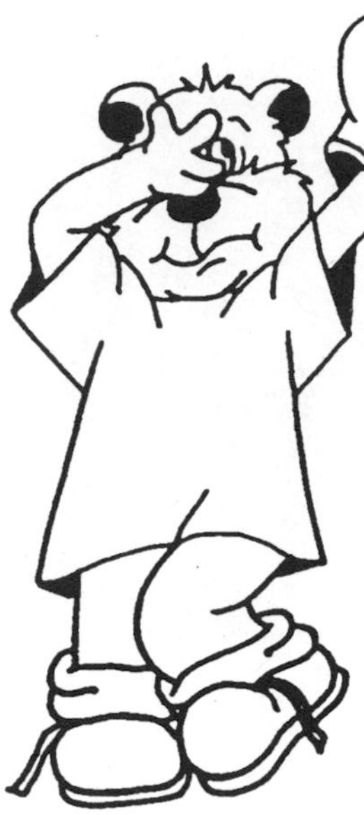

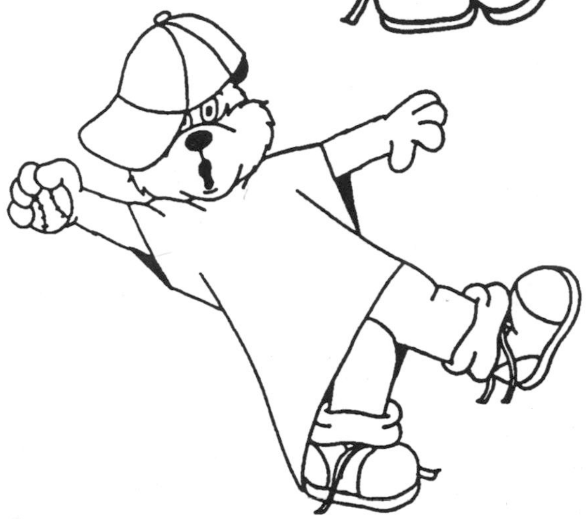

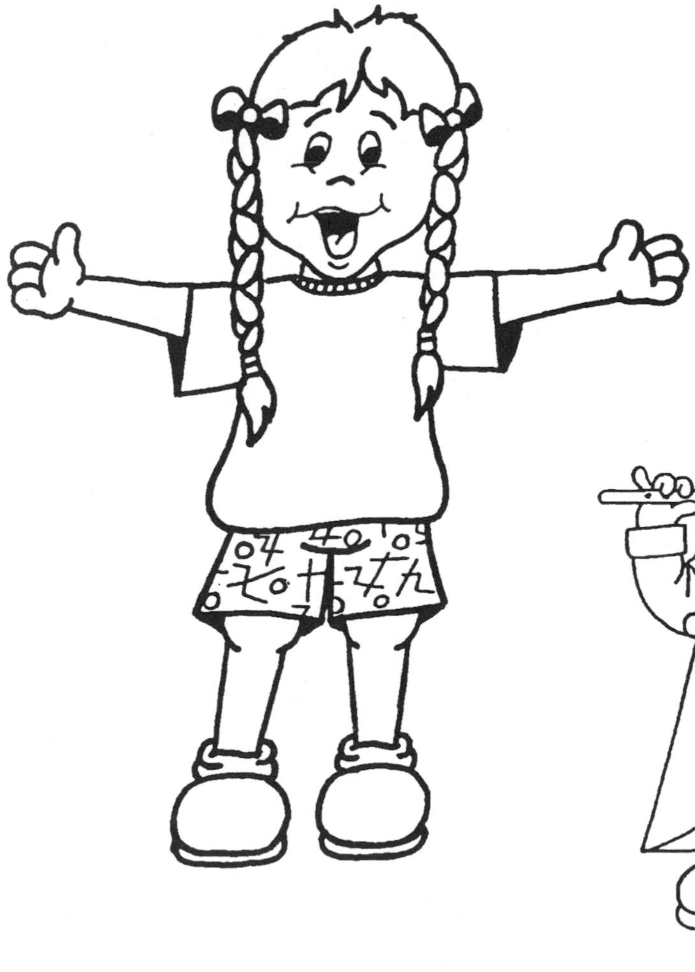

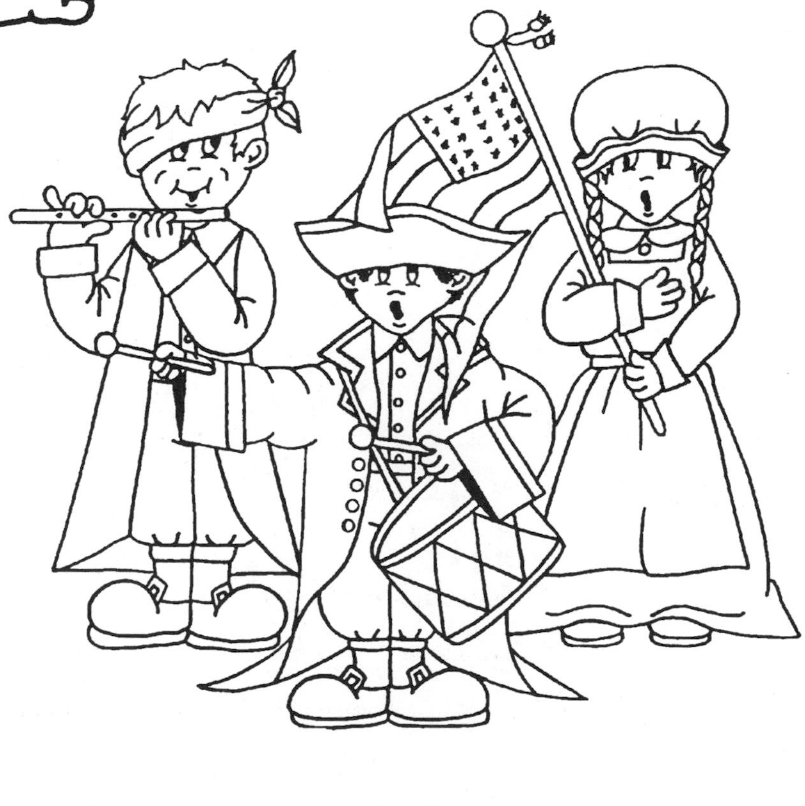

AUGUST ACTIVITIES

August Activities

Name

August

Sunday	Monday	Tuesday	Wednesday	Thursday	Friday	Saturday

CALENDAR ACTIVITIES

Print the following activities on squares of paper the same size as the spaces on the monthly calendar. Have the children cut out the following activity cards and then paste them on different calendar days.

Make a dinosaur footprint in the mud.

Look in your backyard for proof that a dinosaur was there.

Go to the library. Find a book to read about your favorite dinosaur.

Write a poem about a dinosaur.

Tell your parents six facts about dinosaurs.

Build a dinosaur out of papier-mâché.

Make a peanut butter and jelly dino-sandwich.

Pretend you are a paleontologist. List your new discoveries.

Z-Z-Z-Z-Z-Z-Z!

When a dinosaur walks, he shakes the ground,
Knocking down trees for miles around.
When a dinosaur speaks, it comes out as a roar.
It'll break your windows and rattle your door.
When a dinosaur eats, he takes pretty big bites
From bushes and trees or whatever is in sight.
I'm sorry they're extinct and not around anymore.
But can you imagine the sound of a dinosaur's snore?

Knock! Knock! Knock!

They say that dinosaurs died long, long ago
When the weather changed and the world turned cold.
But that's kind of sad, so I'd like to believe
They took off in a spaceship with an alien named Steve.
They're traveling around, exploring the stars,
Or maybe they decided to settle on Mars.
If my theory's right, then they could return
To share with us the secrets they've learned.
So don't be surprised by a knock on your door,
It just might be an extinct dinosaur!

Thump! Thump! Thump!

A dinosaur stubbed his toe on a rock.
It took a week to feel the shock!
When he finally felt it, he cried out in pain,
Then looked around for someone to blame.
Of course, seeing no one, what could he say
Except "Thump! Thump! Ouch!" as he limped away?

Minds-On Fun for Summer © 1992 Fearon Teacher Aids

The Case of the Missing Lunches

This is a play about five dinosaurs who attend Mesozoic Elementary School. Lunches have started missing from the classroom. Everyone is making accusations and jumping to conclusions about who stole the missing lunches.

Cast:
Stegosaurus
Tyrannosaurus Rex
Triceratops
Brontosaurus
Pteranodon

Props:
Lunch sacks
Brownies (optional)

Scene 1

Scene 1 opens with Stegosaurus, Brontosaurus, and Triceratops sitting outside just about ready to eat their lunches.

Stegosaurus: Leaping lizards! Someone got my skunk cabbage and peanut butter sandwich. I was really looking forward to eating that, too!

Brontosaurus: I'll give you half of my tuna and seaweed burger. That is, if Rex didn't already eat mine, too.

Triceratops: Did he get caught stealing again?

Brontosaurus: No, but we all know he did it.

Stegosaurus: You just can't go blaming him. We need proof.

Brontosaurus: What more proof do we need? When you stop to think about it, he's the biggest, meanest, and hungriest dinosaur in school.

Triceratops: Hey! Here comes Pteranodon. What do you have to eat? We're starving! Rex stole our lunches again!

Pteranodon: Here! You can have mine. I'm not very hungry. I had a big breakfast this morning. Hey, Brontosaurus, if you think Rex took your lunches, why don't you go over there and take his?

Brontosaurus: Well, maybe we do need more proof.

Pteranodon: Gotta go, guys! I've got to return a book to the library.

As Scene 1 ends, the three friends devise a plan to catch Rex stealing their lunches.

Minds-On Fun for Summer © 1992 Fearon Teacher Aids

Scene 2

As Scene 2 opens, the three friends are giggling and whispering.

Stegosaurus: Did you do it? Did you? Huh, huh?

Brontosaurus: Sh! Keep it down! We don't want the whole world to know about it.

Triceratops: Well, did you?

Brontosaurus: That was the plan, wasn't it? This is going to be good! I put enough volcano hot pepper sauce on that sandwich to melt an iceberg.

Stegosaurus: This is going to be great! I can hardly wait! How much longer until lunch?

Triceratops: Sh! Here comes Rex.

Brontosaurus: Hi, Rex! Hope you have a big appetite today.

Tyrannosaurus: What do you mean by that?

Brontosaurus: Nothing, except you're the only one who's been eating a lunch lately.

Tyrannosaurus: You don't know what you're talking about! I've got better things to do than talk to you dino-brains.

Brontosaurus: See, told you it was him!

Triceratops: That doesn't prove anything. We're just going to have to wait for lunch and see what happens.

Scene 2 ends as the three friends walk into the classroom.

Scene 3

Scene 3 opens as the three friends sit down for lunch.

Stegosaurus: Well, is it gone?

Triceratops: Bingo! He took the bait!

Brontosaurus: This is going to be good. Now all we have to do is wait.

Stegosaurus: Brontosaurus, are you sure you put enough volcano pepper sauce on the sandwiches? Rex is over there eating his lunch and he doesn't look like he's on fire to me. He should be jumping around like Pteranodon over there!

Pteranodon: Water! Water! I'm on fire! My tongue feels like hot lava.

Brontosaurus: Serves you right! We put hot volcano pepper sauce on our sandwiches to catch a thief!

Stegosaurus: Yeah! And it looks like you're it.

Triceratops: What a mean thing to do. All the time you let us blame Rex!

Pteranodon: It didn't seem to make any difference. You had already made your minds up.

Brontosaurus: Well, this is the last lunch you're going to steal at this school. Someone go get the principal!

Stegosaurus: I think there is one more thing we need to do.

Triceratops: What?

Stegosaurus: Apologize to Rex!

Tyrannosaurus: Did I hear something about an apology?

Brontosaurus: Oh, didn't see you standing there, Rex. Ah, um, we just wanted to say we're sorry for the way we've been treating you and accusing you of stealing our lunches.

Tyrannosaurus: I'm sorry, too, for calling you dino-brains. Let's just forget it. Here, have one of my mom's famous beetle bug brownies!

Scene 3 ends with all the dinosaurs munching on beetle bug brownies and laughing about the hot volcano pepper sauce sandwich.

Minds-On Fun for Summer © 1992 Fearon Teacher Aids

QUESTIONS AND ACTIVITIES FOR THE PLAY

1. What was being stolen at the Mesozoic Elementary School?

2. Who did the three friends think took their lunches? What was the plan to catch the lunch thief?

3. Retell the story in your own words.

4. Have you ever accused someone of something they didn't do? When?

5. The friends were convinced that Tyrannosaurus Rex was guilty of stealing. Examine the evidence they had against him.

6. Evaluate the friends' plan. Did they do the right thing? Why or why not? Make up a plan that you would have used to catch the thief. Compare your plan to the one the characters used. Be specific.

7. Design an invention to catch a thief.

8. Do you think Pteranodon learned his lesson? Explain. Predict what might have happened if Pteranodon had not been caught.

9. Do you think Pteranodon needed to be punished for his crime? If so, what do you think his punishment might be?

10. In your opinion, did the friends take a logical plan of action to catch the thief?

Name _____

Cut out the pictures below and paste them in the correct boxes.

When I went to ☐ , I had a bad dream. It was all about a ☐ from a

☐ that I'd seen. I dreamed he was chasing me and I tripped on a ☐ .

I jumped up and kept running, but my ☐ stuck in a bog. Something grabbed

hold of my muddy wet ☐ . Fortunately, I escaped by the buzzing of the

alarm ☐ . My ☐ and ☐ were at the ☐ of

my bed, and so was the book about dinosaurs I'd read.

shoe   clock   pillow   dinosaur   sock

log   bed   blanket   foot   book

78

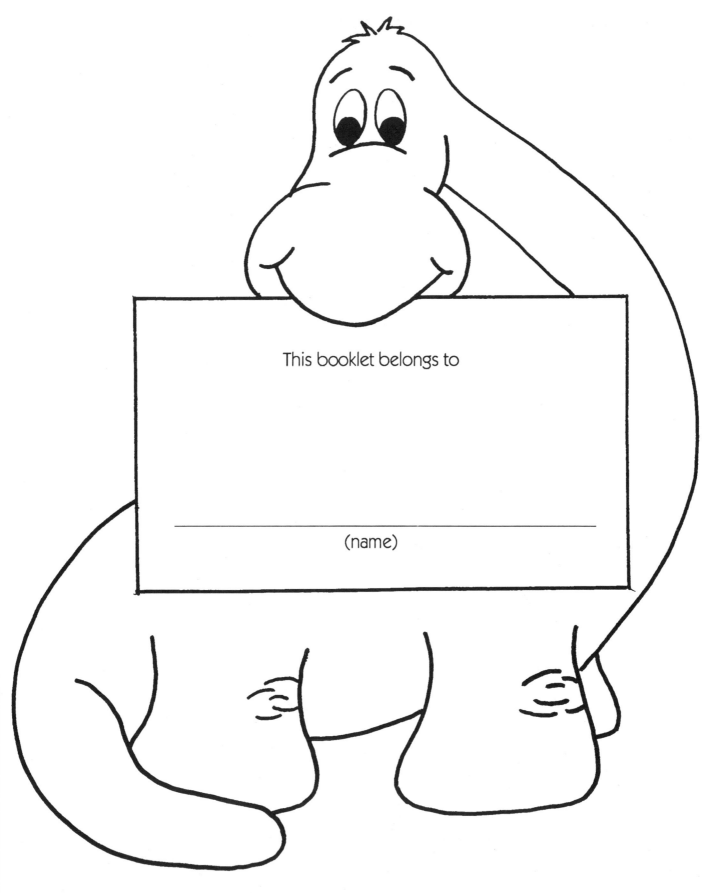

This booklet belongs to

_____

(name)

This booklet belongs to

_____

(name)

Minds-On Fun for Summer © 1992 Fearon Teacher Aids

Name _____

Name _____

82

While working on his field notes
in the museum late one night,
Terry Dackdel, a world famous
paleontologist, heard the rattle of
bones and an eerie cry coming
from somewhere in the building.
Oh, my gosh! It's . . . . . What
happened?

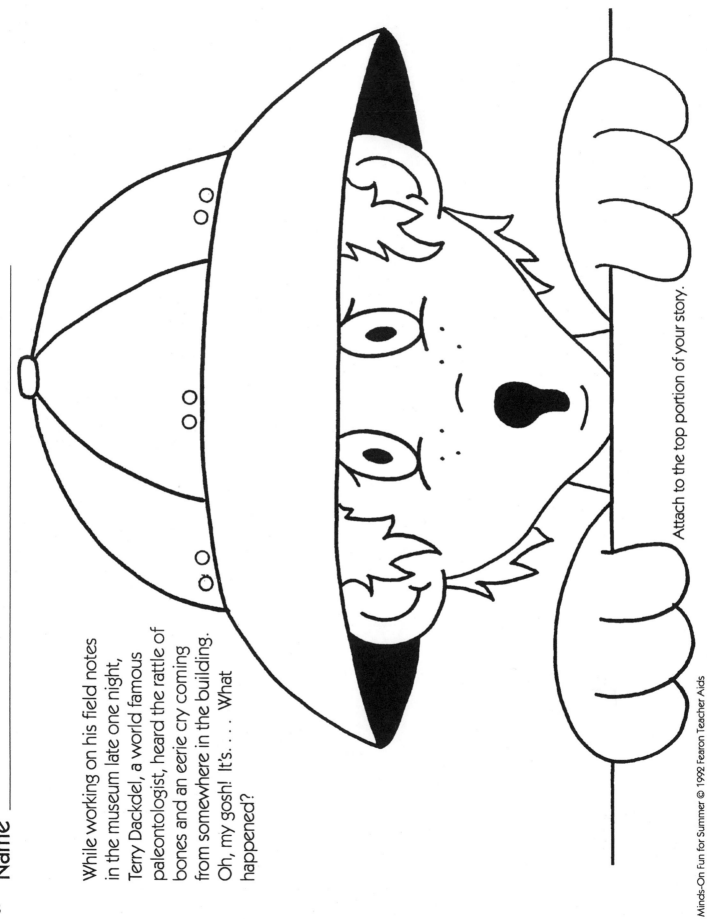

Attach to the top portion of your story.

Attach to the bottom portion of your story.

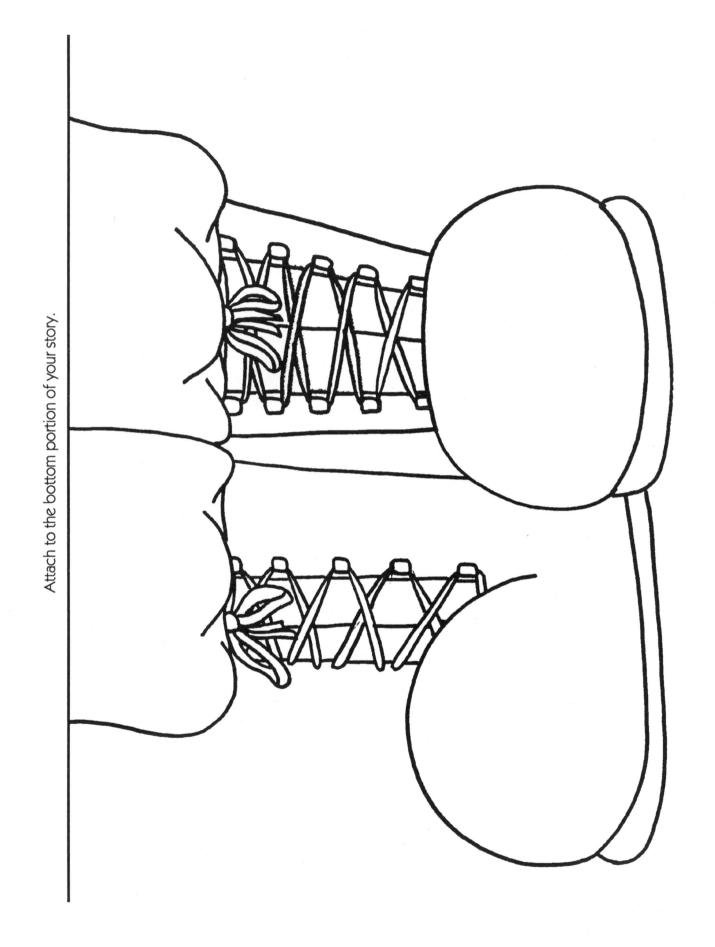

All the scientists don't seem to agree
About why the dinosaurs ceased to be.
Some say the Ice Age wiped them out.
Some say meteors, others say drought.
The earth was changing so much back then.
Who really knows what happened to them?
What's your theory on why they died out?
Or do you think they're still roaming about?

Use your imagination!

_____

_____

_____

_____

_____

_____

_____

Minds-On Fun for Summer © 1992 Fearon Teacher Aids

Name _____

You are cordially invited to submit your recipe for the Third Annual Dine-O-Rama Prehistoric Cook-Off! The prize this year is an all-expense paid vacation to the luxurious resort of La-Brea by the Swamp.

_____
Name of Recipe

1. _____   4. _____

2. _____   5. _____

3. _____   6. _____

_____

_____

_____

_____

_____

_____

Name _____

A group of paleontologists
Out looking for dinosaur bones
Came across a cave
Partly hidden by some stones.
They carefully uncovered the entrance
And took a look inside.
They found ancient picture writings.
They couldn't believe their eyes.
These pictures told a story
About a big dinosaur.
But what was so amazing was
It had never been seen before!

What do you think the picture message looked like? Draw the message.
Translate the pictures into words to tell a story.

Minds-On Fun for Summer © 1992 Fearon Teacher Aids

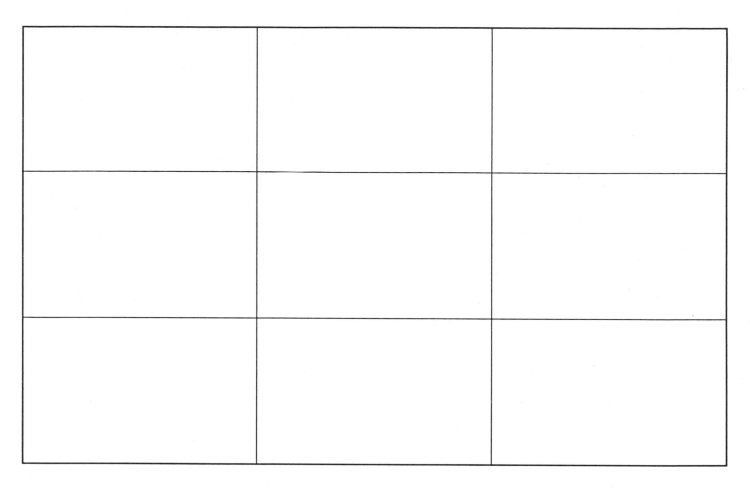

You need to do some research on Stegosaurus. Go to the library and check out a book. Go back 2 spaces.

Whee! It was fun sliding down a Brontosaurus' neck. Go back 1 space and slide again.

You went to the library and got a book about dinosaurs. Move ahead 3 spaces and read it.

 Tyrannosaurus Rex has just spotted lunch—you! Run ahead 2 spaces.

You discovered dinosaur bones. Go back to the museum and assemble them. Lose a turn.

You forgot the vegetables for Hadrosaurs' lunch. Go back 1 space and get them.

You stopped to watch a Stegosaurus hatch from its shell. Run ahead 1 space to tell a friend.

You took a ride on the wings of a Pterodactyl. Move ahead 3 spaces.

The volcano is erupting! Quick! Find a safe place to hide. Lose a turn.

Minds-On Fun for Summer © 1992 Fearon Teacher Aids

Name _____

Name _____

Name _____

_____
(child's name)

did a "dino-might" job in school today!

_____
(teacher's name)

Leaping Lizards! !

_____
(child's name)

_____

_____

_____
(teacher's name)

Minds-On Fun for Summer © 1992 Fearon Teacher Aids